HEALTH HELPERS

I NEED A DENTIST

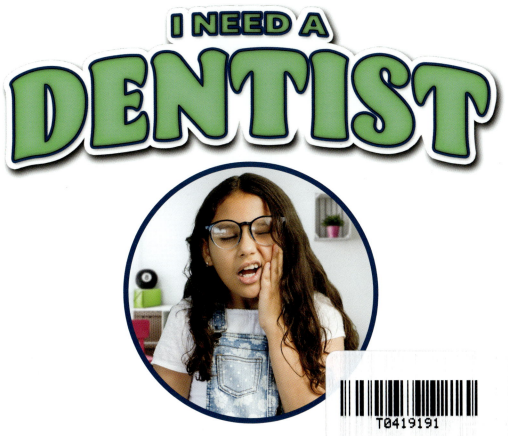

By Rachel Rose

Consultant: Beth Gambro
Reading Specialist, Yorkville, Illinois

BEARPORT
PUBLISHING

Minneapolis, Minnesota

Teaching Tips

Before Reading

- Look at the cover of the book. Discuss the picture and the title.
- Ask readers to brainstorm a list of what they already know about dentists. What can they expect to see in the book?
- Go on a picture walk, looking through the pictures to discuss vocabulary and make predictions about the text.

During Reading

- Read for purpose. Encourage readers to think about the kinds of things that might make us need a dentist.
- Ask readers to look for the details of the book. How can a dentist help?
- If readers encounter an unknown word, ask them to look at the sounds in the word. Then, ask them to look at the rest of the page. Are there any clues to help them understand?

After Reading

- Encourage readers to pick a buddy and reread the book together.
- Ask readers to name two things they might find at the dentist's office. Find the pages that tell about these things.
- Ask readers to write or draw something they learned about dentists as health helpers.

Credits

Cover and title page, © Photographee.eu/Adobe Stock and © AntonioDiaz/Adobe Stock; 3, © Mariia Vitkovska/iStock; 5, © Pixel-Shot/Adobe Stock; 7, © ruizluquepaz/iStock; 8–9, © SeventyFour/iStock; 11, © JackF/iStock; 13, © Dmytro Zinkevych/Shutterstock; 14–15, © xavierarnau/iStock; 16–17, © shironosov/iStock; 19, © peakSTOCK/iStock; 21, © Lorado/iStock; 22TL, © Med-Ved/iStock; 22TR, © choness/iStock; 22ML, © Oleksandr Sadovenko/iStock; 22MC, © Tohid Hashemkhani/iStock; 22MR, © Nigel Stripe/iStock; 22BR, © andresr/iStock; 23TL, © asbe/iStock; 23TM, © Pixelimage/iStock; 23TR, © Prostock-Studio/iStock; 23BL, © LeviaUA/Adobe Stock; 23BM, © OPEN.TESM/Adobe Stock; 23BR, © 5D Media/Adobe Stock.

See BearportPublishing.com for our statement on Generative AI Usage.

Library of Congress Cataloging-in-Publication Data

Names: Rose, Rachel, 1968- author.
Title: I need a dentist / by Rachel Rose.
Description: Bearcub books. | Minneapolis, Minnesota : Bearport Publishing
   Company, [2025] | Series: Health helpers | Includes bibliographical
   references and index.
Identifiers: LCCN 2024021936 (print) | LCCN 2024021937 (ebook) | ISBN
   9798892326322 (library binding) | ISBN 9798892327121 (paperback) | ISBN
   9798892326728 (ebook)
Subjects: LCSH: Dentists--Juvenile literature. | Dental care--Juvenile
   literature.
Classification: LCC RK63 .R67 2025 (print) | LCC RK63 (ebook) | DDC
   617.6--dc23/eng/20240702
LC record available at https://lccn.loc.gov/2024021936
LC ebook record available at https://lccn.loc.gov/2024021937

Copyright © 2025 Bearport Publishing Company. All rights reserved. No part of this publication may be reproduced in whole or in part, stored in any retrieval system, or transmitted in any form or by any means, electronic, mechanical, photocopying, recording, or otherwise, without written permission from the publisher.

For more information, write to Bearport Publishing, 5357 Penn Avenue South, Minneapolis, MN 55419.

Contents

A Dentist Helps 4

Dentist Tools 22

Glossary 23

Index 24

Read More 24

Learn More Online........................ 24

About the Author 24

A Dentist Helps

My tooth hurts.

Ouch!

Who can help me?

I need a dentist!

> Say dentist like DEN-tist

5

The dentist office is busy.

I have to wait.

Then, it is my turn.

The dentist takes me to a room.

My dentist is very nice.

They help me sit in a big chair.

It can go up and down.

The chair can tip back, too.

Wheee!

The dentist puts on a **mask**.

They wear **gloves** on their hands.

This keeps us safe as the dentist works.

Open wide!

The dentist looks in my mouth.

A little **mirror** helps them see every tooth.

Is this the one that hurts?

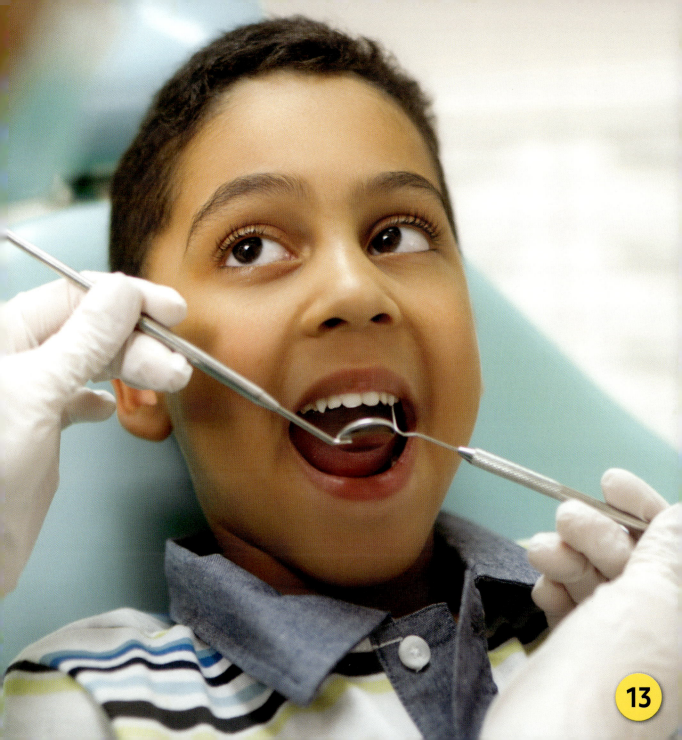

The dentist takes an X-ray.

This is a picture of my mouth.

It shows the insides of my teeth!

Uh-oh!

I have a small hole in one tooth.

The dentist says it is called a **cavity**.

They need to fill it in.

Say cavity like KAV-i-tee

I am a little **scared**.

But the dentist gives me some **medicine**.

It helps me feel better.

19

Now, we are done.

That was fast.

My tooth feels much better.

Thanks, dentist!

21

Dentist Tools

A dentist uses many tools.

- Gloves
- An X-ray
- A mirror
- Medicine
- A dentist's chair
- A mask

Glossary

cavity a hole in a tooth

gloves hand coverings

mask a covering for the nose and mouth

medicine something taken to stop sickness or pain

mirror a piece of glass that shows what is in front of it

scared feeling afraid

Index

cavity 16–17
chair 8
gloves 10
mask 10
medicine 18
mirror 12
teeth 12, 14, 16, 20
X-ray 14

Read More

Birdoff, Ariel Factor. *Dentists (What Makes a Community?).* Minneapolis: Bearport Publishing Company, 2022.

Cipriano, Jeri. *Going to the Dentist (My First Time).* Egremont, MA: Red Chair Press, 2022.

Learn More Online

1. Go to **FactSurfer.com** or scan the QR code below.
2. Enter "**Need Dentist**" into the search box.
3. Click on the cover of this book to see a list of websites.

About the Author

Rachel Rose loves to smile, so she takes great care of her teeth and gums!